Shining Star

Also by the author:

The Singing Road

Going On

Shining Star

by Nora Beth Main

The Naylor Company
Book Publishers of the Southwest
San Antonio, Texas

Library of Congress Cataloging in Publication Data

Main, Nora Elizabeth, 1885-
Shining star.

Poems.
I. Title.
PS3525.A4154S46 811'.5'4 75-14150
ISBN 0-8111-0581-4

Printed in the United States of America

Dedication

May the Lord protect and keep you
May your children love you too
May the God of heaven guide you
On your walk with men
May His loving care surround you
May your friends be kind and true
May the peace of heaven bless you
Till the year rolls 'round again!

Contents

The One Invisible

The One Invisible 1
Hold Fast Your Star 1
Windows 2
The Great Aristocrat 2
My Country 3
Survival 3
Morning Star 4
Our Country 4
Our Children 5
A Dad's Good-bye 5
Citizenship 6
Sing a Song of Friendship 6
Good Citizens 7
We the People 7
Acquiring Poise 8
Peace of Creativity 8
The Mighty Pen 9
Power of Truth 9
Labor 10
Greatness 10
Courage 11
Tolerance 11
Human Nature 12
Garner State Park 12
God and Science 13
Remembering 13
Burdened Lincoln 14
Emblem Eternal 14
The Ministry 15
Easter – Grace of God 15
Sonnet to Giving 16
Reclaiming Guam 16
To Change the World 17
Sonnet to the Jesus Way 17

Out of the West

Out of the West 18
Valedictory 18

Frontiers 19
Mystery 19
Singing Hills 20
Nocturnal Soliloquy 20
Seeing God 21
Reminiscence 21
God and Man 22
Thy People, Lord 22
Invincible Courage 23
Land of the Free 23
The Untried Year 24
Fairest Builder 24
Anticipation 25
Vernon Centennial 25
God or Greed 26
To Dr. James R. Bunch 26
The Hour Has Come 27
Sonnet to Kemper and Crew 27
The Way 28
Surcease 28
The Shut-in 29
The Only Way 29
Quiet 30
Nocturne 30
What Peace 31
Living Hope 31
The Great Centennial 32
Armistice 32
Greatness in Fellowship 33
The Eternal 33
Organ Music 34
Hearts that Fail 34

And What of Years

Years 35
Word Power 35
Kismet 36
Shining Hour 36
A Teacher's Soliloquy 37
Pantomime 37
The Desert Blooms Again 38
Lesson 38
This I Preach 39
The Sacred Soil 39
Faith 40
Heart's Reward 40
Swish 41

Sonnet to Myrtle Thomas 41
To Princess Margaret 42
Perspective 42
Sonnet to Eighty Years 43
The Roundup 43
Warren Loy 44
To Vyola Hubbard 44
Maynette Baldwin 45
Game of Life 45
Inevitable Harvest 46
Potentiality 46
Mystery 47
Boomerang 47
Enduring Happiness 48
Always Tomorrow 48
Soliloquy to Inwood 49
Unceasing Reminder 49
Compensation 50
New Year Calling 50

The One Invisible

The mighty searchlight sends its swinging ray
Thru fog and mist too dense for human eye . . .
The lamp streams wide, in circular display
Unveiling secret haunts of earth and sky.
A lighthouse stands within the breakers' roar
As raging billows strain to crash the beam,
While driven ships, too near the rocky shore,
Hug tight their lanes led by the steady gleam.

Lighthouses, searchlights, give them any name;
The One invisible on land or sea
Is that unfailing, everlasting flame,
Which lights the path for all humanity.
Its warm soft glow delights the weary soul –
A pilgrim's beacon – long as the Ages roll!

Hold Fast Your Star

Dedicated to Rev. B. L. Brown

Your star may seem to hide behind a cloud
But it is always there to point the way;
It's never far when you are in a crowd,
Just keeps on sending down its perfect ray.
You marvel, watching, as the slender beam
Spreads out – into a glamorous design –
A fiery flair, a scintillating gleam
To touch your life anew, with God's own shine.

When God made stars to light the sky at night
He must have looked down centuries to be
And found that millions, gazing in delight,
Were always looking up, and sensed their glee.
God loved the stars – they sang for Him at dawn;
Your star is God's own Light, to lead you on!

Windows

Dedicated to Mrs. B. L. Brown

The early Day Star flames thru mists of time,
And watching from my window on the sky
Dawn's a capella, singing ancient rhymes,
Salutes – while deep night shades go marching by.
The mists of shimmering and tossing night
Spring into space, to spread a golden glow –
Awakening mankind to Heaven's Light
And blessings, open windows may bestow.

The Star! Each dawn it flashes in again!
What joy, could we but fathom its return . . .
At daybreak all the living world may learn
Life's truest meaning, from the silent plea.
When dawn's immortal lettering appears –
God's Word becomes our window on the years.

The Great Aristocrat

He handled wood and tools! His mind was keen.
He lived close to the Lord to learn His truth . . .
He built a body very strong and lean –
And traveled miles to be baptized – a youth.
From that day on he walked the open road –
Taught love, to ease the bitter hate and fear . . .
The doubting rabble followed his abode,
And marveled at the words they came to hear.

Not born to wealth but noble heritage
More noble than a mortal man may know;
A carpenter, as learned as a sage
With all the wisdom Heaven could bestow –
Altho he died upon a huge cross-tree
He lives – that we might live, eternally!

My Country

Enshrouded in the mist of centuries
My Country — rugged, primitive and grand —
Lay subtle and sublime, between the seas,
The wild swift strength of nature in command.
The soft print of a moccasin is seen
As Redskins roam their free untrammeled way,
Till sharp illumination strikes their dream —
It is the dawning of the white man's day.

There is no backward trek from any foe
When men of truth and justice march along . . .
They build a Nation as they sing their song
And keep the torch of Liberty aglow.
My Country — built by races of the earth —
We offer thanks to God, who gave thee birth!

Survival

Since early times America has faced
The enemies of all her hopes and schemes —
When strong uncompromising forces raced
Against the lifeline of her freedom dreams.
No ideology could quite compare
With harmony of life from every shore . . .
Endowing thought and impulse and such rare
Design as lampshine at our country's door.

Today we ponder danger's gravest threat —
Since fearless pilgrims praising God alone
For free land such as they had never known,
Pledged loyalty we never shall forget.
What now, can break the pattern of our cause,
When its design was fashioned from God's laws!

Morning Star

A new horizon breaks upon the way . . .
The slender fingers of approaching dawn
Reach toward the console of the sky, to play
A morning song, as night's grey shade is drawn.
The nation's mortals synchronize their lot
And listening bestir their hearts to rise . . .
Join in the song and be the patriot
No human mind could ever quite devise.

It must not be that man shall close the book
Put out the light and finish his brave dream . . .
Nor ever lift his eyes again to look
At God's fresh dawning and a bright new scheme.
There is a new horizon where you are
When you can think to flag the morning star!

Our Country

The claim of birth is my inherent right
To everything America holds dear . . .
To all that IS my country, in its flight
Thru darkened skies to reach the sunny clear.
Since first the golden door stood wide ajar
And that straight beam swept out across our way,
Men knew that God had raised a guiding star
Whose brilliance would suffuse the world some day.

This land has been a constant proving ground,
A refuge and salvation from despair . . .
With new designs for living that abound
For builders of a wondrous thoroughfare.
And we have shared with all humanity . . .
The song of peace and truth that makes men free!

Our Children

What matter if a lad is out of tune
A-whistling as he pedals down the street!
The birds are whistling too, as it is June
And summer sends her call for little feet.
A deep green lawn like velvet carpet laid,
Where tiny children scamper, almost nude;
A fancy bucket, little rake and spade
Work charms while mother gets an interlude.

The twilight finds them sprawled in snowy beds,
Their suntanned bodies lost in dreamless sleep . . .
They never have to toss their curly heads
For slumber comes before they count a sheep.
Dear God, we love our carefree youngsters so,
What kind of world will they grow up to know!

A Dad's Good-bye

I saw a wondrous, fleeting glance flash on
And felt as if I rode a speeding train –
Now it was here, now swiftly it was gone,
Yet, this parental gesture was not vain.
It suddenly released a hidden sheen
Upon the features of a patient face,
And I shall not forget that I have seen
Shine forth, the secret glow of kingly grace.

This flash portrayed a love he would not sell
Should wealth of countless centuries unfold,
Though poverty and hunger weave a spell
To sever this relationship for gold.
A child had set in motion, on the run . . .
A precious dad's "good-bye" to his small son!

Citizenship

Within the heart of every foreign-born
Are hopeful words well hidden from our eyes,
Yet they were etched indelibly that morn
When flamed ideas sped across the skies
And we shall need a finer vision . . . set
For things invisible, and keener sense,
To read this living glowing novelette
Personified by longing and suspense.

But there is none save God can read such truth,
Such yearning of the soul to be let free;
Such dreaming of a country in his youth . . .
Such peace, when dreams become reality.
This newfound peace is hard to understand
For native sons inherit their great land!

Sing a Song of Friendship

Come, sing a song of friendship true and brave,
The virile kind, that knows no severing . . .
The ties may strain and lengthen as they cling,
Yet do not snare nor make of one a slave.
But make your song of friendship sometimes grave,
And sometimes gay . . . a gracious lively thing,
To run the gamut of the scale . . . and wing
The melody upon an endless wave.

I know that when a hearty friendship song
Goes caroling around the Hemisphere . . .
Its message will encircle hearts, along
The ramparts of defense afar and near;
For when you sing a song of friendship true,
Its friendliness will echo back to you!

Good Citizens

How can I number all the truly great . . .
The millions who pursue such kindly ways,
Disdaining prejudice and futile hate,
Whose daily living is a hymn of praise!
They are the little people of the land
From everywhere across the broad domain,
Whose noble virtue lifts the weary hand
Of him whose burden is the greater strain.

Wherever courage wanes and anguish starts,
Church chimes intone their Angelus to prayer
Reminding of God's peace in human hearts,
And sanctuary from temptation's snare.
Who would be great let him deserve the name,
Though small the niche or heightened by acclaim!

We the People

How lightly we regard that noble phrase
Or fail to note the import of its role . . .
We see it often and consider ways
In which its genius seeks a peaceful goal.
"We," somehow, seems to mean the government,
The industries, the organized array
Of timely groups, that leave us quite content
As progress hangs its banners on display.

But we, the people, work a magic charm,
A righteous freedom, to ennoble man
And train him to become his own strong arm . . .
To give his voice, his vote, for such a plan.
And even die, that liberty be saved,
Since death were better than a life enslaved!

Acquiring Poise

We read and speak of changing times, of when
Tomorrow comes and we can prove our worth . . .
And speculate upon a regimen
Or policy, to feed the poor of earth.
Nor would we hesitate at sending aid
If in the doing we preserve a land . . .
Yet wisely, and with candor, unafraid
And brotherly, should we extend our hand.

Christ moved with dignity and gracious strength
Without a show of fear or cold pretense . . .
So too, may we walk down our Nation's length
Renewing Christian pride, and common sense.
Unmoved by rivalry on paths untrod . . .
Remembering, the world belongs to God!

Peace of Creativity

The boon of mass invention in our age
Designs a way of living for itself,
And not entirely pleasing is its page
Delineating on the title, "Pelf."
Not that possession of the lucrative
Is vain or prodigal, but something fine,
Inscribed to man so long as he shall live,
Nor ever to create a golden shrine.

Arrayed in wealth above a mortal's dream
The lily rises from its bed of earth . . .
Toils not, nor spins, as man who toils for worth,
Who earns his gift, held for a time, supreme.
And lest man weary of his daily fare . . .
God sends a gift of lilies, for his care!

The Mighty Pen

God, may I always think, before I write,
Remembering that printed words go far;
That I am not infallible, that might
Of flaming pen may consecrate or mar.
Let me be thankful for the right of print
And never, to proclaim my views, deride
My countrymen offensively, nor hint
Ironic prejudice, that may divide.

I would remember that some distant day
My words, returning, in the mind and heart
Of man, may bear the fruitage of decay,
And bow me to the dust for my poor part.
So, I would use my pen constructively,
To mold the mind of man, to keep man Free!

Power of Truth

Some tour and write, or follow other lines
Or learn a native language far from home;
Some ply a trade or work in jewel mines
While others plant deep roots and cease to roam.
But precious as these labors are to each
And valued as they seem, a truth remains;
That in their midst, where missionaries teach,
Grim shackles fall and broken are the chains.

When centuries of ancient teaching cling
Like grappling steel, to subjugate man's will
The missionary speaks of greater things
And weaves a miracle of "Peace, be still."
The storm of life subsides, the shadows fade —
Dawn flames and man breathes free and unafraid!

Labor

To labor is the varied work of mind,
Of heart, of hand, and very soul of man;
All these concur in one gigantic plan
To fashion habitation for mankind.
And none is worthier since he designed,
Nor is it more to ply with skill a span,
Or build a shining roadway for a van . . .
Each one will find his noble work enshrined.

If towers tall reach up to touch a star,
All are the nobler toilers of the host . . .
And if broad acres planted yield their part
No worker's praise is heralded afar . . .
Nor is it good that mortal man should boast
Save that to labor is immortal art!

Greatness

How warmly thrilling just to stand within
The aura of a person truly great . . .
To feel that glowing presence permeate
And fill the emptiness that takes us in.
How radiant that selflessness, to guide
The spirit into clearer streams of thought
Where miracle of vision freshly wrought
Sweeps littleness before its cleansing tide.

How much of greatness wears a neat disguise,
Content, remotely hidden from the crowd.
To fling its ribboned light thru dismal skies
Long after death has modeled its grey shroud!
So great is greatness, we may sometimes learn
That there's too much of it to quite discern.

Courage

If zest for living falters in the flight,
Not only will a writer live to write,
But die a little as each forming line
Inscribes the ultimate in life's design.
Not only will a mortal travel far
To scan the heavens for a shining star,
But delving deeply into pits of gloom,
Will find a jewel in a dusky room.

If thoughts become a coverlet of dark
As embers hug their evanescent spark,
And dawning seems a million hours away,
Tomorrow will provide another day,
For God keeps vigil from the realms above
To send a gift of courage with His love!

Tolerance

So little gained by negative appeal . . .
For every ear is turned toward harmonies
That vibrate and awaken, and unseal
The caverned depths, to set the heart at ease.
A worthy message whether song or word
Expands to higher, finer realms of thought,
And inspiration, as the tones are heard . . .
Then hearts are mellowed and refined and taught.

But if a truth is preached convincingly
And proved a truth, as it is given voice,
Its value could decrease, by enmity
Against the freedom of another's choice.
The right of worship is a human cry . . .
If that be lost, our peace would surely die!

Human Nature

It's easy to be serious, today . . .
Sarcastic even, as the burdens press;
The hectic swiftness seems a roundelay
Which drowns our quiet peace and happiness.
The little cares and worries bear us down,
The ordinary trials dissipate
Our energy, and etch a telltale frown . . .
And we feel cheated, carrying such weight.

We whine and get depressed, and lose our song
When bitter disappointment stalks our trail,
But human nature fights its way along . . .
Quite certain, in the end, right must prevail.
Renewing, resting, laboring . . . always,
The keen, exciting struggle . . . in relays!

Garner State Park

Majestic! Mystic as the bluish haze
That drifts across the chiseled peaks, with sheen
Tinged golden in the twilight glow. The day's
Departure drops a mantle . . . on a scene
Created by the Great Omnipotence!
Descending shadows drape the canyoned walls,
While gentle Frio sleeps to night-bird calls . . .
And down the centuries, comes, recompence!

They come and go . . . the curious! And feel
Exalted . . . more than flesh and blood and bone.
They are a part of this . . . the truly real;
Each for the other made . . . man finds his own.
Adversity . . . unfolds a regal plan . . .
Which waited ages, for the touch of man!

God and Science

Our faithful doctors labor thru the years
To stretch the life-span longer than before . . .
To keep man living, overcoming fears
And gaining strength beside his own front door.
No need to be forever anxiously
Preparing for that dreaded voyage now . . .
Just meditate upon longevity
As man's concern for man gives life, somehow.

And Man's concern has given man a goal . . .
To gain abundant life . . . as God decreed,
To loosen chains of bondage, be made whole
Not half, but Man emancipated, freed!
The Lord asks only that we worship Him . . .
To live life freely to the golden brim!

Remembering

It's good to set apart a timely date
Remembering some person or event,
Reviving principles to emulate . . .
Reliving glory splashed with wonderment.
And it is well that days be put aside,
Ring-marked each year, upon a numbered sheet,
Yet, mortals are reluctant to abide . . .
Forgetting that remembering is sweet.

Beset by every labor man must share
He lets important days go fleeting by . . .
And if no day made citizens aware,
Our sacred memories could fade and die.
Our Country's God set Freedom's lamp aglow,
Each one remembering . . . will keep it so!

Burdened Lincoln

Top-hatted, weary, rather stately tall . . .
To Lincoln, these were days of great alarm,
Young patriots were answering the call
And watchers wept in pity at their charm.
The fighting men in tattered uniforms
Sang bravely as they prayed, and here and there
Above the battle noise and thunderstorms,
Heard voices joining on the cold night air.

And what of gnawing hunger, what of pride? . . .
They loved to eat – wear garments fitted well,
But singing, marching, paining deep inside
If they should fight their kin, saints would rebel.
As Lincoln blotted at his tear-filled eyes
His love for all men seemed to crystalize!

Emblem Eternal

Is any soul within this Freedom Land
Near to surrendering his liberty . . .
Near following false forces that command
A subtle way of life . . . to bind the free!
Is there one cold embittered personage
Within the borders of America . . .
Near blotting out his Christian heritage
With evil's proud, austere anathema!

If such were true, that Freedom's song might end,
And sacred institutions fail and fall,
That, inconceivably, our wills would bend . . .
How quickly we'd alert in vibrant call,
We'd sing and write and teach the living world,
That Freedom's Flag be evermore unfurled!

The Ministry
Nora and Warren

I never shall forget the day I stepped
Along that center aisle, to volunteer
My life for God – without a trace of fear . . .
I cast my plans and treasures down, and wept.
My ship went sailing safely o'er the sea –
My compass had been set, by heart and soul,
In any climate steering for a goal
A beacon pointing toward Eternity.

Then on the way, another climbed aboard!
Someone to share his love and heart's delight
And from that day the two of us have soared
Thru heavenly realms with victory in sight.
Our ministry together – none can tell,
Yet, hosts of Christians know, and all is well.

Easter — Grace of God
Dedicated to the late Rev. W. P. Deatherage

The lofty carillons break forth in song;
Old melodies are flying thru the air –
We join – wherever holy words belong
While millions worship God in silent prayer.
The wondrous Earth hangs quietly in space
Ignoring clamor and discordant din –
But thru the torment comes "Amazing Grace,"
The steady clarion call, to cease from sin!

The same high clarion sounds for us today
In vibrant peals, entreating all mankind,
In all the troubled world, to pause, and pray
For lasting peace, good will, and tranquil mind.
The golden answer to the world's discord –
In loving and revering Christ the Lord!

Sonnet to Giving

Dedicated to the Berean and Victory classes and Woodlawn Christian Church

The heart's good gifts are moved by love, we know,
Some different as daylight and the dark –
But Christian love is touched by Heaven's glow
Which never fails to leave a shining spark.
We cannot count the varied signs we see,
The countless gifts far past our numbering,
God's attributes that bless humanity –
For these – our thankful Hallelujahs ring.

Sometimes the lesser gift will be the gleam
To light the way along a rugged road . . .
Yet, every gift we share with friends can beam
For others, till they reach that loved abode.
Receiving gifts – my cup of joy o'erflows
How then is it "more blessed to give" – who knows?

Reclaiming Guam

The vanguard of the Free, a few Marines,
Look out upon the far Pacific blue
And love the sea, and all its varied scenes –
Lone sentinels, they scan each wave and hue.
Out where a star becomes a friendly guide
And moonlight spreads a carpet for their feet,
The song of Waters sweeps in with the tide
Immortalizing freedom, and the Fleet.

Then all the grandeur and the heritage
Is blasted with the flame of human guile
And brave young heroes meet the sudden rage
But write their names in blood each losing mile.
This, the avengers read, as tho a Psalm . . .
And raised, again, Old Glory over Guam!

To Change the World

A super-star is hanging high and bright,
'Tis Christmas, Shepherds watch their snowy sheep.
A mountain lion creeps along at night
In search of some safe place in which to sleep.
But that is here in our America –
Not on the sands of ancient Bethlehem,
Yet in a sense it seems a replica
Of sacred Truths from which our blessings stem.

The brilliant star, the shepherds, Angels too,
And singing from the sky of One whose birth
Would bring Salvation to the realms of Earth –
Untarnished outlook – Life forever new!
How long, how long shall blest humanity
Resent the living truths, that set men free!

Sonnet to the Jesus Way

Now we desire to retroactively
Recapture and restore the fire and zeal
That motivated hearts and set them free,
To preach the Truth which Jesus made so real.
The word of God became alive in ONE
Who walked with men, and taught the human race
That they become immortal thru God's Son,
That Life Eternal is a gift of grace.

And each became a Temple spirit filled,
With Holy power to cleanse the world of wrong,
Forever walking in the Way God willed . . .
The Jesus Way . . . of righteousness and song.
Now let it come, this cleansing from the past,
Step in, the stream of Life is flowing fast!

Out of the West

Sky towers builded in a distant sky
Reflect the living glory that is each . . .
Our streamlined car tho fashioned miles away
We drive in pomp to hear the parson preach.
The smoke-draped cities know the touch of skill
As toilers' craft creates a million schemes . . .
And sky-clear towns with tall trees hushed and still,
Are lavishly adorned by far-off dreams.

We garner what our hands have never sown . . .
Accept as due the progress genius made,
And wear the mantle as it were our own
Tho blood and tears had stained its fine brocade.
"Am I my brother's keeper?" stirs the mind . . .
To stark proximity of all mankind!

Valedictory

All over this great land, the ranks of youth
Are marching down that long awaited aisle . . .
They have learned discipline and living truth;
Now, capped and gowned, they walk the sacred mile.
Loved ones and loyal friends watch breathlessly
The handshake, and the proffered slender scroll,
As each proud graduate accepts the fee . . .
That heightens value and delights the soul.

They bid farewell to vaulted ivy walls,
Or leave a smaller school with hearts aglow. . .
Or stadium, where thousands from the halls
Of city schools join ranks, erect and slow
Soon . . . all America will move along
To their clear voices leading Freedom's song!

Frontiers

Not long ago the round world seemed so large,
And distances so great . . . then ships set sail,
To conquer oceans wide and deep, a charge
Which only brave men dared, and must not fail.
Adventurers were driven by a force
But few men knew, and some went out for gold,
While others sought to ply a magic course
To treasured vastness wilder lands might hold.

America, a frontier dream come true . . .
A dream of freedom and democracy,
Shall ever be a frontier for the new
And untried, undeveloped liberty
In science, education, art . . . and God,
For all are potent, as the lush green sod!

Mystery

"The earth is flat," they said, then it was found
Through careful scientific figuring . . .
That it was very like a globe and round,
Which truth itself was not so heartening.
For there remained such depth of mystery
That no man, to this day, can comprehend
The moving cosmos to a great degree . . .
Nor tell what luminosities portend.

The mysteries of Life are God's alone . . .
Yet, when the quickened mind is sensitized
To scientific truths but vaguely known
And step by step a dream is realized . . .
Discovery is made! It is God's plan,
Then science leaps again, ahead of man!

Singing Hills

Eternal hills, how gallantly they live,
How grandiose their muted symphony! . . .
Our lives are awed by their serenity,
Our ardent natures made less combative.
The elements arrayed as warriors
Are stilled before their strengh and quietude,
Are hushed into a passive interlude . . .
Subservient before their conquerors.

Among the crested hills the night winds run
The gamut of a sweet Aeolian . . .
As night birds trill their tunes in unison,
And lull to sleep the tired eyes of man.
A day and night among the singing hills
Is worth a lifetime of a city's thrills!

Nocturnal Soliloquy

The ambulating moon moved down the sky
As if to preen superiority,
Before such models as propose to vie
In swinging round the earth's periphery.
Her brilliance gave no hint of countless miles
That march thru time to flash a friendly glow –
Nor was the bouffant robe disguising wiles
With borrowed glamor from a daytime show.

If she could speak, would there be praise for us,
That our small moons could orbit outer space
And send back signals to the human race –
With speed to make the beauty envious!
Were earthlings first to send up satellites –
Or others somewhere, like our precious mites!

Seeing God

At last, man looks upon the firmament
And ponders every wonder in surprise . . .
Till now he had been earthy and content
To let astronomers survey the skies.
The handiwork of God was sacred lore –
Beyond him, out of range, and off the path
His feet had trod, and never would explore;
Now he must ponder a strange aftermath.

He sees his own small plot as very choice
But finds his world horizons antedate . . .
And hears the challenge of his Country's voice
In every flying Flag, and quells his hate.
Then suddenly a bright new orbit gleams
And he sees God . . . in man's immortal dreams!

Reminiscence

Once, wagon wheels rolled rumblingly along
The winding trails where countless dangers lurked,
And some remember still, the wild weird song
Of open range life where they planned and worked.
The vision comes again as they recall
The fire of pioneer adventuring –
The feel of horseflesh, sound of hoof, the bawl
Of cattle – then wet eyes, remembering.

Like wagon wheels, the centuries have rolled
Their rumbling way along the trail of years . . .
And Ages broke their silence when the bold
Adventurers laughed lustily at fears.
They flung a shining star into the sky . . .
Then gave their blood, that Texas might not die!

God and Man

So long as human ingenuity
Stirs up a waking world to search for Truth,
The vast frontiers of nuclear energy
Will need the genius of our growing youth.
With toys as modern as the satellite,
Excited small ones ponder and compare
The intricate designs . . . then fly a kite
To watch its wondrous antics in midair.

So long as nature's vast horizon beams
Its phantom ray toward some enchanting star,
Someone will ply its bright auroral streams
In search of Infinite spectacular.
The Lens is trained on realms beyond our sky,
God's outer space . . . for man to glorify!

Thy People, Lord

Quite early in my childhood the imprint
Of all the world began to form for me . . .
Seems I have always known of that fine stint:
Be neighborly, unprejudiced and free.
I'd like to step across the border way
Of every nation on the living earth,
Learn how they'd like to live and work and pray
And how they'd act if freedom could have birth.

No shadow of a question that mankind
Of every race and color has been blest,
And, could each know the other, we should find
That God still loves us all, and none the best.
Our Youth when far afield keep home alive . . .
But where they go, romance and friendship thrive.

Invincible Courage

Some places I have lived loom hauntingly
Upon this lone horizon where I dwell,
The kind familiar faces turn toward me
And every heartbeat chimes a vesper bell.
Dear ones long wed now share grandchildren's joy;
Their many pictures bright with happiness
Come caroling that time cannot annoy,
If I still cherish friendships I possess.

But intervals are lengthening between
As time walks up the narrow path of years,
And friends may step across the earthly scene
Where Heaven's dewdrops are the only tears.
Heartache and longing for the ones away . . .
Break on the near and distant shores today.

Land of the Free

Amid the turmoil of a war-torn world
There is a place of refuge left for man;
One mighty fortress with its Flag unfurled,
Its torch held high for all the earth to scan.
From dawn, to blazing noon . . . to eventide,
Old Glory's flare becomes a sentinel;
Reflecting Heaven's own pure light, to guide
A Nation's steps, to guard a citadel.

Above the roar and scream of Europe's din,
The sound of marching, drilling feet is heard,
As young America . . . to undergird
The Nation's strength, reports for discipline.
O Land of faith and love and Liberty,
You shall prevail . . . and stay forever Free!

The Untried Year

The bleak unknown can bring a chill to some,
A cringing, at what seems futility . . .
Fatigue, at burdens only minimum,
A shudder at the future, groundlessly.
Yet, every untried day must have its dawn,
Must break with promise for the trusting heart . . .
Must grant high courage and the might of brawn,
To nurture faith to face a fresh clean start.

No vantage point is gained in fearfulness,
For love and laughter are the spirit's guide . . .
To every trusting soul the load is less
And bright horizons flame, if faith abide.
We put our trust in God to banish fear . . .
And meet with confidence, the glad New Year!

Fairest Builder

Life's made of dreams, the dreams that live and grow,
For finest dreams left idle fade and die . . .
How many are the lost we cannot know,
But everyone has let a few pass by.
When talent dreams no longer fascinate
And creativity has ceased to prod . . .
Our silent weariness cries out too late
As others climb the heights while we must plod.

Dreams turned to embers may flare into flame
And nourished quickly may become a blaze,
May light creatively the torch of fame
Even beyond the bearer's earthly days,
If dreaming wakens any gift at all
And God is donor, no gift is too small.

Anticipation

Now comes the spring, to ease the winter pain –
Or so it should be spring, yet on its glide
Around the yearly carrousel, in vain
It strives to catch the brass ring, yes it tried.
Daylight dreams on and lingers in the chill,
As one surmises truant spring has fled . . .
For snow falls and the wind whines weird and shrill
And flowers sleep beneath a soft white spread.

Next time the music stops and spring descends
Perhaps the sun will smile a welcome glow . . .
While human hearts find joy as winter ends,
And spring puts on her gayest fashion show.
If only spring could sense the tiresome wait,
She would arrive on time, and never late!

Vernon Centennial

The century has spent its hundred years
To count among the many that have flown,
Yet there is none to tell of pioneers
Who braved the dawning of that vast unknown.
Not one who looked along that earthly span,
Could vision such fulfillment of a dream
As blossomed when the century began . . .
And none discerned our love and high esteem.

Could they have visioned what tremendous change
The century would fashion for our day . . .
The swiftness of our lives might have seemed strange
And their own primitive, the better way.
But they bequeathed their glowing faith to us,
And made the century victorious!

God or Greed

Wise watchman on the world's periphery
What is the signal from that far-off shore . . .
Does it reveal the Man of Galilee
Upon the wild sea's dashing waves, as yore?
What is the signal flashing now, to you . . .
Do fearful hearts betray our tragic need
As mounting billows rise and rage anew,
To dash our craft against the rock of greed?

Brave watchman on the world's perimeter
Is there no star to chart our stormy way . . .
Are beating winds the only leveler
To whip our spirits into calm, today?
He will respond, if we have faith to cry . . .
He'll calm the storm, lest faithless we would die!

To Dr. James R. Bunch

He was a truly dedicated soul
Who never faltered in the time of strain,
And wanted only to pursue his goal
To ease anxiety and lessen pain.
He carried well his own deep suffering,
His days of sorrow no one else could share . . .
The silent days, perhaps disheartening,
From which he always garnered strength to spare.

He could have lived life less courageously
While others minister as time grew brief . . .
And in the shade of his own vine and tree
Lose all the glory of his loved belief.
Unto the end of days he'd serve and give . . .
There was no other life he wished to live!

The Hour Has Come

The hour has come! The darkened sky has flamed!
The sky we hoped would let the sun shine thru;
The peaceful, brilliant sky, that long has framed
Starshine and sifted gold, within the blue.
The hour has come . . . and we have felt the blow;
Stabbed in surprise and treachery . . . it fell
In sudden lightning crashing, screaming shell —
And rich warm blood of patriots let flow.

The hour has come, but we are not afraid;
United as a solid rock . . . we stand,
A nation that shall never be dismayed:
For God, and home, we lift a mighty hand.
We pledge our lives against the enemy,
And raise our flag for true Democracy!

Sonnet to Kemper and Crew

The men of science fly a sacred course,
Dip to the stars and rend the silent veil —
Tall dreamers driven by a hidden force
Fly up the lone untried celestial trail.
They bend their wills to shape a destiny,
To guard the portals of a glorious land —
Concede to none save God, who set us free
And placed a guiding lamp in Freedom's hand.

The blue calm glides into a stormy lane,
Beguiling hope from every gallant breast,
As Death, in wild abandon, rides the plane
To barter sacrifice for holy quest.
Poor proud slayer . . . only the mission ends,
They shall live on, remembered by their friends!

The Way

There is no peace a mortal may possess
Until the principles of Truth ordain . . .
No freedom until love is free to reign,
For love and truth are born of righteousness.
Truth is the living spirit to do good:
In place of cruelty, love rules supreme . . .
And will abolish every evil scheme
Until God's peace for man be understood.

The simple teachings of our Lord are pure,
So that no man may fail to learn and heed . . .
Till righteous peace prevail and hold secure
Against the enemies of human need.
So shall we ever pray, and be one mind,
To bring the way of Truth to all mankind!

Surcease

A poet spends long fruitful hours to find
The color combination for a phrase,
To strike a portrait on a reader's mind . . .
His careful technique hidden from the gaze.
Then other hands pick up his precious work
To linotype and print . . . and it looks well,
But when the poet reads he spies a quirk,
A gremlin spelled a word as he would spell.

And all the hours and all the skill are lost,
For one lone letter changing thought and style
Becomes a devastating holocaust . . .
At least, a poet's heart has died awhile,
But Time the spender, Time the mender flies . . .
And every little heartache somehow, dies!

The Shut-in

The shut-in may feel lonely-lost awhile,
As those unmindful of the better years
Continue in the pattern they would style –
Yet none should be alone, God knows and hears.
When from a distance comes a note or card
Or lengthy letter with a wealth of news,
Or poems written by a friendly bard –
All life's drab colors change to gayer hues.

Those friendly people once aglow with charm
Have names recalled less often than before . . .
For life is swift, in town and on the farm
And all the world seems just outside the door.
But they have time to travel everywhere . . .
With note or poem, or a book . . . for fare!

The Only Way

The future leads down one lone path to peace,
And may not seem quite smooth enough at times,
When steep and rugged mountain trails increase
The strain of weary miles and chilly climes.
But there's no highway quite so glorious . . .
None where a holy King has paved its length,
Where signals on the trail are luminous
To guide our walking and renew our strength.

Today, we touch our torch to His bright flare
And gather glory to suffuse the hate
That rages in the world where some despair . . .
Where some know not the King we celebrate.
There's room enough for all along this road
And all the world may find a safe abode!

Quiet

There's beauty in the quietude of space
Where blue skies canopy the silent trail,
And stir the heart to purity of grace . . .
Unknown where din and clamoring assail.
There is such freedom to reflect the true
Where mountains lift their grandeur heavenward,
And man is quieted and cleansed anew . . .
Far from his canyoned walls where sight is blurred.

And there is wonder in the quietness
That permeates the depth of quiet eyes,
The leveler, to free the soul of stress . . .
To lay a mortal bare of neat disguise.
But my imagination fails to phrase
The saintly quiet of the Master's gaze!

Nocturne

The brilliant moon lit up the purple hills,
The silent peaks read Psalms and sang a hymn,
Creation's Master tuned the rippling rills
In obbligato to the seraphim.
Symphonic echoes touched a snowy steep,
Rebounded far across the radiance
Vibrating, blending, coloring . . . till sleep
Crowned man and beast, in humble circumstance.

In distant dimness evening stars proclaim
Nocturnal blessings on a tired world,
Their chantings rival in celestial fame
The song of morning stars as dawn unfurled.
In holy resignation man is blest . . .
As Heaven puts the weary earth to rest.

What Peace

"My peace," the Master said, "I leave with you";
Yet in our bent to capture place and power . . .
In puny wishfulness we misconstrue
The dignity of peace in its full flower.
Had He not said "My peace," we might have thought
That peace came by the world in which we live,
For certainly within this world was bought
At highest price, the peace He seeks to give.

"My peace . . . not as the world gives," He made plain;
Nor fear, nor trouble, nor the strife of hate
Can kill the soul; the evil strive in vain
To lave the mind in streams that desecrate.
Peace is the greatest category still . . .
Scheme to replace it . . . nothing ever will!

Living Hope

Dedicated to Rev. Bob and Cherry Chandler

If hope could speak, and loose the deafened ear,
Could stir again the dormant life to dream
And sing of love and courage down the year . . .
That would be miracle enough to scheme.
But when all of life is burdened overmuch,
When faith grows faint and careless of its need,
Hope will avail . . . thru kindly human touch
To share its melody of word and deed.

Over the world a freedom spirit wings –
It is our song of faith and hope in flight;
Out where the dark is deep it broods and clings
Till dawning hope dispels the gloom of night.
There's glory in a hope that shares the good
To build a world of Christian brotherhood!

The Great Centennial

The tread of time steps to a measured beat
Resounding down the trail of centuries . . .
There is no turning back, no sharp retreat
To wait the passage of hostilities.
The century has traveled down our way
Reminding of the rugged trackless years,
When faith and vision planned a better day
Than fate presented to the pioneers.

Now we who stand upon the borderline
Envision murals round the living earth . . .
With simple dignity and truth divine
Portrayed in thoughts and deeds of matchless worth.
The future flings her challenge toward the goal
And all our names are carved upon the scroll.

Armistice

I cannot quite respond to Future Peace,
Nor cold financial status kept or lost,
Nor that Cease-Fire may bring a draft decrease –
My thoughts are anchored to the bitter cost.
I cannot quite erase the stricken hills
Which once gave quiet strength to shelter life,
Where rugged height lent solace to man's ills
And proffered benediction – never strife.

And yet, for battered peaks I do not moan
Save for their littered plight – the blood-let cry
Emerging from each mass of flesh and bone
Where once tall courage flamed, nor sought to die.
For freedom – that last day they fought and prayed –
The wounded, dying, living – they have paid!

Greatness in Fellowship

The call of God came steadily and clear –
Down corridors of mind the echo rang
Until a world made desolate by fear
Took up the cry, as faithful women sang.
It pierced the hymn, the Psalm, the fervent prayer –
Caught up in Christian Fellowship, its plea
Became the voice of women everywhere
As God's horizon flames, and dawn breaks free!

God's call still comes in steady high refrain
That women's hands, once bound, point out the way,
For poignant as the first high scream of pain
The world's deep need of God is heard today.
While sounding now, from Fellowship's tall tower
A call for greatness strikes the needy hour!

The Eternal

What is this life, which enters on a cry
And leaving, slips away so quietly . . .
This proud intangible that will not die,
And rides the wind on every stormy sea!
The years between – the brave years and the best,
Are touched by shadows on the daily goal . . .
And braver hearts that travel on the quest
Would not, to gain the world, give up the soul.

There is no price a mortal may command –
No value quite enough to compensate
For mysteries we do not understand,
But shall, at that wide-open golden gate.
Surpassing all our ways and sacred lore,
This life has chosen Life forevermore!

Organ Music

An ancient monolith bereft of trees,
Is warm and living, in its holy place . . .
Its carved-out pipes fling ageless harmonies
From silent keys where spirit fingers race.
In reverie beyond a mortal's fare,
All day and thru the night until the dawn
Uplifting as a mountain's purest air . . .
The sound of organ music lingers on!

I know a sacred organ balcony
Where chambered silence waits the human hand,
Where touch of human fingers real and free
Finds breakthrough to that far Eternal strand.
But whether fantasy or Church so dear . . .
This much we know: God must be very near!

Hearts That Fail

There is a rumbling in this plot of Earth
The people murmur, murmur constantly
What is the happening, what is the dearth
That crowds upon us until none can flee!
No one can fathom its approach, it seems,
When suddenly the milling clouds are squalls
Which threaten life and freedom, until dreams
Come tumbling down like dashing waterfalls.

God's world has rugged paths and thoroughfares
Where varied mortals whom he also made
Keep pushing to the front, in their affairs
And they should reach the top, if not delayed . . .
Now while our Freedom Flag still waves and waits,
Trust God . . . our valued coin reiterates!

And What of Years

Years

Years hold a chalice of the love of God,
The overflowing cup for every need . . .
And they are measured by a magic rod
Held out to signal triumph as they speed.
Years are the distances we journey by
And beckon onward at each flaming dawn;
They are the labor and the poignant cry
That every life begins and ends upon.

Years are the messengers that run beside
With light and truth to shape our destiny;
They mark the trend from morn till eventide
And set the pace along eternity.
Years are as finite as our own small sphere
And infinite as God's eternal year.

Word Power

The one most needful of a ray of cheer
Is often cheated, often lost to sight
By those most amply fitted and quite near . . .
Till one day cold hard earth subdues the plight.
Someone may carry in the soul till death
The heartache only kind words could dispel,
Could ease the weariness, the slow of breath . . .
Words . . . in the spirit of Emmanuel.

Some words have power to kill . . . some cut away
Life's dreary curtain letting love shine in.
For with this sharpened weapon man may slay
Or save a life, or sever earth from sin.
Kind words leap into life to paint a scene
Like golden apples on a silver screen!

Kismet

I often think of John and his last days
Upon the Isle of Patmos growing old,
As mortal reckoning besets his ways
And ties of other years slip from their hold.
When distance spreads unyielding miles between,
Did gentleness reach out for tired hands
Now weak from toiling long at harvest glean . . .
Did none perform the commonest demands?

I think of early martyrs crucified,
With few to help them bear the agony
And few to watch an hour or stand beside,
Alert, to minister unfailingly.
Why dream of favor when the hour chimes late,
While one is least – and they God's truly great!

Shining Hour

The brightest hour that came to humankind
Came when the night was darkest over earth,
When long forgotten prophecies stood blind
Before the shrouded hour of Jesus' birth.
When all of Life was bleak and barren waste,
The Lord wrought nobly as the heavens rang . . .
And shepherds fled Judean hills in haste
To search for Him, of whom the angels sang.

It is the story of the Ages now . . .
The hallelujah of that shining morn
Flames up anew each day, as mortals bow
And bless the hour that God's own Son was born.
It is a shining no man can erase . . .
No dark of night can hide the Saviour's face!

A Teacher's Soliloquy

When I look into eyes that look toward mine
And speak to ears that listen searchingly,
I sense a hungering for things divine . . .
And yearning hearts are asking this of me.
I sense their longing for a brighter way
Where only truth and righteousness can lead . . .
And suddenly the words I planned to say
Seem quite inadequate for such a need.

Then swiftly I look up toward God, and reach
For thoughts illumined by His matchless beam . . .
And find the answers on the face of each
As learning sets their questing minds agleam.
So, for my teaching, Lord, one thing I ask . . .
That I seek wisdom for this noble task!

Pantomime

If it be green or white we shall not care
For Yuletide is the time of mirth and joy . . .
With gifts and goodwill wishes for our fare
We travel far to see a baby boy.
We ride the years to distant Bethlehem
To bring our gifts as Wise Men long ago,
For pillowed in the starshine like a gem
The tiny Christ Child sleeps within the glow.

Adorned in brilliance from a strange new star,
The small town teeming with a tired throng
Is heedless of the angels and their song . . .
The crowded inn or stable door ajar.
The scene has traveled down the years to us
Forever living and victorious!

The Desert Blooms Again

I saw the rolling, blowing endlessness
Where sands cry out their thirst in awesome tones . . .
Where wild winds whip and whirl, and send distress
To pillage that strange peace, the desert owns.
The restful desert calm – the chosen way,
Is broken by the tragic turbulence,
But one can feel beneath his feet the play
Of unrelenting forces in defense.

The fertile seeds dig deeper into earth
Lest fiercer winds blast thru their treasured hold
And foil the radiant glory of new birth –
The floral coloring Life would unfold.
At last the tempest hurls a drenching rain
To cool hot sands, and ease the pregnant pain!

Lesson

The dizzy clanging carrousel I ride,
The never-ending, rounding gypsy whirl . . .
While words flit by, "In me abide,"
And other words that blur, seem to unfurl.
"Be still and know that I am God," and pray;
The living Word speaks and I should rejoice,
But I reply that I've no time today . . .
The busy grind drowns out my needful choice.

Then suddenly I'm thrown free of the round
And I resent the sudden painful shock . . .
Yet, prone upon this cot I hear no sound
Save one small whisper and a gentle knock.
As certain as I shall rejoin the din,
I shall remember Heaven's discipline!

This I Preach

There is what seems the proper way, I know . . .
Yet I alone must choose, for I am free!
I only am the judge, and be it so
Until the Judge of all may pass decree.
I would not strive against my countryman,
Yet, I, a soldier, bear a sharpened sword,
And I must use it as I caravan
My pilgrimage among the countless horde.

Two-edged and sharp, the weapon I may fling –
Not made of steel, though it will cut away
The chains of sin to give the spirit wing –
And God Himself commended this affray.
He gave the weapon – Word of God – to teach,
To change the heart – to free it – this I preach!

The Sacred Soil

Wherever I have touched the mystic loam
And whether north or south or east or west . . .
I plant my heart roots deep and build a home
Upon a little plot, and love that best.
Yet, I keep dreaming of another place
Where first my bare feet ran along a lane,
Slipped into puddles, muddy-streaked my face
While playing Indian and wagon train.

Now, looking down the long swift row of years
I feel the soft warm soil between my toes,
And see thru dimmer eyes the splash of tears,
The quaint mud pies and splotches on my clothes.
Red, black, or tan, just any kind of earth
Is sacred, if it's from the land of birth!

Faith

Faith is a word of mystery and awe,
Without which all vocabularies fail . . .
Inadequate to cope with life and law
And every weighty problem with detail.
Faith is a word to lift man out of sin,
To set eternal music echoing
Above the ageless human battle din . . .
Its blatant turmoil harsh and deafening.

Only the quiet deeper channels hold
The answer to the empty nets, it seems,
For surface waters cannot quite enfold
The treasure in their shallow swifter streams.
So pull away from mankind's barren shore . . .
Surprise awaits where faith yields up her store!

Heart's Reward

Hearts were not made for scheming, nor for guile;
Nor can one bear the constant drip of hate
That some must bear, and strive to quench the while,
Lest fibers weaken and capitulate.
The brave heart sends its beat against the goad
That strives to drive its dart into the soul
And often wearies of the heavy load . . .
And prays that God may make the sinner whole.

Christ is the only hope for hearts that bleed –
He knew humiliation and defeat,
And by that crisis met the world's deep need –
By His atonement, life was made complete.
The heart of all mankind yearns for the day
When dark of sin has lost its power to sway!

Swish

There go the women of the yesteryear
Brave to the last quaint ruffle on a skirt . . .
They never knew of worry, nor of fear,
But riding far held tightly to a quirt.
I cannot reminisce to a degree,
Nor vision nature's gift of loveliness
To rich and poor alike, for courtesy . . .
The miracle surviving toil and stress.

I've never heard that any lacked the cash
For purchasing a bolt of shining fluff,
With yards of lace for trim, and velvet sash . . .
When calico was not quite style enough.
And at their fortitude we catch our breath –
Yet on our highways they'd be scared to death!

Sonnet to Myrtle Thomas

No more shall slender fingers play along
Piano keys in rhythmic mystery . . .
Till hope is born . . . till music of a song
Made holy by her touch, shall dwell with me.
No more to feel her gentle charm and grace
Ennobling lives, inspiring them to sing,
Till hymns of worship fill the sacred place
Where God is guest, and Allelujahs ring.

No more to watch the wonder of her skill,
Esteemed and praised by every loyal friend . . .
Yet, fond remembrances revive at will
A presence, so divine, it cannot end.
The moving spirit of her earthly life
Shall dwell with us and mellow all our strife!

To Princess Margaret

The world admires the loveliness of one
Whose friendly spirit is a lilting song . . .
Quite unrehearsed it springs from depths begun
In childhood, learning right instead of wrong.
And how adorable that ecstacy . . .
Cascading over countless lives and schemes
Like cleansing, healing waters . . . suddenly
Reviving faith in their remembered dreams.

Her youthful charm and grace unmoved by fame,
Her sympathetic, understanding heart –
Like breath on embers – kindle into flame
The zest for life that plays a nobler part.
For she has answered life's exacting call . . .
Come as it may, in service great or small!

Perspective

They seldom lift their eyes to mountain tops
Once glorious in fir trimmed finery . . .
And most alluring when the twilight drops
Its purple curtain over sky and sea.
They miss the beauty and cascading roll
Of nature's organ in profundo swells,
To ease the senses and rejoice the soul –
They have forgotten where such wonder dwells.

Some have no mountains, no deep oceans near,
But friends and loved ones always in our sight,
Once famed and cherished, may become less dear,
Should we forget their wonder and delight.
Too much of nearness may impair the view
Without God's love to keep it ever new!

Sonnet to Eighty Years

Dedicated to Mae Elkins

While all your friends and loved ones celebrate
And tell of memories they hold most dear . . .
Sweet, patient, time stands at the garden gate
Humming a happy tune to wish you cheer.
May every birthday be the happiest
And every gallant year ride swiftly by . . .
And may you claim each day the very best
As twilight tints the far horizon sky.

Birthdays are milestones, every one a gem –
The fleeting years creating as they go
A priceless treasure for a diadem,
Worn only in the light of Heaven's glow.
And when that one, great birthday comes along,
Angelic choirs shall sing their greatest song!

The Roundup

What price . . . this freedom we enjoy today!
'Twas purchased . . . but the debt is still our own,
And it was bought at too great price . . . to pay.
Blood bought . . . and never can the years atone
For hardships keener than our modern ken,
Which knows but ease and comfort, speed and flight.
They're living now, in memory of when
Sharp arrows pierced the air by day and night.

The end of Time would find our debt unpaid . . .
For thus bequeathed to us, is freedom's cost;
And thus the strong foundation laid,
And thus the battle won, and kindred lost.
Round up the remnant . . . pay them honor due . . .
Old-timers, step along . . . the DAY'S for YOU!

Warren Loy

In our small world of battles men have lost,
As mortals view the struggle, yet he won . . .
And yielded every vestige of the cost
As lifting up his life beside God's Son.
And surely often, had petitioned Him
For faith to conquer, and a place to fill . . .
Or drink the cup, so bitter to the brim,
Consigning every drop to Heaven's will.

He lived among us as a trusting friend . . .
Beloved and cherished by his family
Whose constant care and favor were to lend
God's mercy, even to Eternity.
Someday the meaning will be crystal clear . . .
And every battle scar shall disappear!

To Vyola Hubbard

How many times the twilight hour sped by
To drape an ebon robe across the night . . .
How many were the years that seemed to fly
When came a day we looked, and saw a light!
And soon that radiance began to grow
Until it warmed the hearts of everyone . . .
Years raced along, and ageless seemed the glow,
Like ageless faith in God's beloved Son.

Then suddenly the shining dimmed awhile . . .
We measured days by waiting its return,
Yet life is measured not by tear or smile
But inner flame, that cannot cease to burn.
A living flame, thru all Eternity . . .
That leaves its radiance with you, and me!

Maynette Baldwin

The measure of her worth, we may not see!
We look . . . and there stands virtue unafraid,
Transcendently bereft of masquerade . . .
Her soul, a lamp . . . to shine eternally.
Nor pain, nor sorrow, nor fragility . . .
Can dim the brilliance of the cavalcade
Of reminiscent years, met undismayed . . .
Nor hush the holy hymn, of victory!

With finite eyes, we look upon her worth,
And marvel at such courage, to possess.
We sense the purity of heart and mind,
The overflow of radiating mirth . . .
And know, that back of her resourcefulness,
Is faith in God, and love, for humankind!

Game of Life

The game of Life is played to win, or lose;
A hard, exacting game, at any time . . .
Immensely fascinating . . . if we choose,
Exhilarating as a mountain climb.
It can be made a game of give and take;
Exciting, dangerous, adventurous . . .
Or casual and drab, without a break
To mar the dull routine. It's up to us!

However we may play this constant game;
If carelessly, or balanced by a plan . . .
If unperturbed, or surfeited by fame;
It chalks a certain destiny for man . . .
And fairways are not made for solitaire,
A complicated world is playing there!

Inevitable Harvest

Beneath the bludgeonings of fate, the bold
Of earth cry out against the lustful stride
Of ignorance, which leaps like fire, to fold
Within its flaming mantle, seared and dried,
Humanity's bright dream of Liberty . . .
Now bent beneath its blighting weight . . .
Now staggering . . . they never yield . . . but flee
The stark stupidity of fervent hate.

A harvest marches on the soil, where seed
Develops thoroughfares around the earth.
The soil! The seed! The harvest! If a weed
Stands tall and strong . . . may we expect a birth
Of roses from the stem? So, peace comes, then,
As peace is PLANTED . . . in the hearts of men!

Potentiality

Down in the human depth of everyone
Is hidden treasure struggling to be free . . .
Some dormant talent waiting restlessly
To play its role when dawning has begun.
Ensnared, yet longing for the warmth of sun,
For God's bright air to quicken energy
That life and growth might find maturity . . .
This trapped thing fights against oblivion.

If each could know the secret of release
For good creative forces as they plead,
How altered might our way of life appear,
How gifted be the genius to make peace . . .
Out of the dawn would come a flying steed,
The rider crying "Freedom," loud and clear!

Mystery

The leaves are falling on the lawns today . . .
Bright yellow, golden, shades of bronze and red;
Some green ones waiting long for frost, turn gray
As nature's artist slumbers in his bed.
From hilltop curves breathtaking vistas preen
Their loveliness to feast our hungry eyes . . .
And everywhere that frost has etched a scene
We'll gaze adoringly, until snow flies.

The naked limbs quake as the silent rush
Comes drifting down the sky in graceful ease . . .
They lay a forest rug deep-piled and lush,
Though mostly in our yards smoke fills the breeze.
But nature's balance lies beyond our ken . . .
Where life finds death in dust, and blooms again!

Boomerang

Intimidation is the deadliest
Of all the wily sins that blight and bruise,
And strips the perpetrator of his best . . .
Though it escapes him that he, too, must lose.
The crafty one knows agony of fear
As though he wrestled a ferocious beast . . .
For this vain evil yields no crop of cheer
And of the victim's yield, it is not least.

So artless is his guile he cannot hide
The wary thrust that punctuates his pride;
Nor tourniquet the sudden dripping scar
For boomerang is brazen and bizarre.
Of all the sins that God must truly hate,
It is the temper to intimidate!

Enduring Happiness

If happiness were but a pleasant smile
That were indeed an art to cultivate,
For some count smiling culture quite worthwhile,
A lovely camouflage for any fate.
Yet, happiness is not a mood to wear,
A mask to don, a trait to conjure charm . . .
Though mood and mask and trait are passing fair
To shield the personality from harm.

But there's a happiness which lives thru strife,
Immune to fear and endless bickering . . .
A happiness that breathes Immortal Life
That lives in us, and trains the heart to sing.
A happiness . . . to barricade the soul
Lest evil persevere and steal the goal!

Always Tomorrow

When hours drag slowly toward the eventide
And every little care seems heavier,
Life's vibrant interest and zests subside,
And evening finds a heart the wearier.
Then winging far across the treelined space
Day's beauty flings its final colors out . . .
A shining coverlet of sheerest lace
To shame a mortal and dispel his doubt.

Then I am thankful for the velvet night
To ease the weariness in peaceful sleep,
Depending on the morrow's breaking light
To shine upon a pathway not so steep.
Tomorrow, I shall cease to grieve and mope,
For always there's tomorrow with its hope!

Soliloquy to Inwood

How peaceful and secure, that once was brave –
All that was mortal sleeps now in its bed,
All that was pain shall nevermore enslave
Nor ever shall become disquieted.
The ecstasy of labor I once knew
Has webbed a shining gift of golden strands –
A mantle – fallen on the early dew,
As tasks I loved reach out for other hands.

Great Master of Immortal Text, I come,
A student and a learner let me be . . .
For I have added up earth's little sum
And would enroll at Life's Eternity.
I've no tuition, no high sacrifice . . .
But I have kept a lustrous Pearl, for price!

Unceasing Reminder

Time now for Angelus to sing her song . . .
To fling the soft sweet tones upon the air,
The golden tones, that keep the spirit strong
Remembering to pause in silent prayer.
The world is wide and high, and many sounds
Are heard in clangorous discordant din,
But thru the torment one clear note abounds
In steady clarion call, to cease from sin.

The Angelus is ringing out today
In vibrant peals, entreating all mankind,
In all the troubled world, to pause and pray
For lasting peace, goodwill and tranquil mind.
The golden answer to the world's discord,
Is loving and revering Christ the Lord!

Compensation

Life feels a gentle slipping at the moor –
The cherished years of service must have end –
Yet, pleads its loved commission may endure
Until a shining bark sails round the bend.
For if one drop the talent he should use
Regard its living flame a futile ray,
Blind to the finger pointed to accuse . . .
What shall a man report to God one day!

So, gifted life keeps bravely to its task
Selecting from the store that which is best,
Though not a pauper he will humbly ask
For spirit riches to complete his quest.
Remembering . . . a crown awaits the wise
Who live and love and labor for the prize.

New Year Calling

They say I'm growing old, and should not try
To measure talent by the former years,
That I must be content to dignify
These walls where I reside, and shed no tears.
My work is finished, I must not complain . . .
This inactivity is quite the best,
This waning strength from devastating pain
Is but the price of long entitled rest.

Provincials cannot always comprehend
A heart's devotion to the World's affairs,
Or teaching Truth until life's day shall end –
That all earth's children may become God's heirs.
The New Year calls – I hear and see and think . . .
Why should I push myself right off the brink!